GALAXIES

GALAXIES

S E Y M O U R   S I M O N

MORROW JUNIOR BOOKS
New York

This truth within thy mind rehearse,

That in a boundless universe

Is boundless better, boundless worse.

—ALFRED LORD TENNYSON

"The Two Voices"

Printed in Italy

1   2   3   4   5   6   7   8   9   10

Library of Congress Cataloging-in-Publication Data
Simon, Seymour.
Galaxies.
Summary: Identifies the nature, locations,
movements, and different categories of galaxies,
examining the Milky Way and other known examples.
1. Galaxies—Juvenile literature. [1. Galaxies]
I. Title.
QB857.3.S56   1988   523.1′12   87-23967
ISBN 0-688-06184-2
ISBN 0-688-06184-0 (lib. bdg.)

PHOTO CREDITS
All photographs courtesy of the National Optical Astronomy
Observatories, except page 5, the University of Arizona/Steward
Observatory, pages 6, 7, and 32, the U.S. Naval Observatory, and pages 8 and
9, the Jet Propulsion Laboratory (California Institute of
Technology)/NASA. Artwork on page 12 by Warren Budd.

On a clear, moonless night, you can often see a hazy band of pale light stretching across the sky. This luminous band, called the Milky Way, is made up of millions and millions of stars. These stars are so far away from Earth that the tiny points of light blend into one another and you see only a faintly glowing ribbon of light.

Even a small telescope reveals the awesome numbers of stars that make up the Milky Way. But the Milky Way is only part of the two hundred billion stars that make up the Milky Way galaxy, also called just the Galaxy. Even though the stars look close together, the Galaxy is mostly empty space. If a dozen tennis balls were spread out across the United States, they would be more crowded than most of the stars in the Galaxy.

The bright streak in the photograph is the track of an artificial satellite from Earth that happened to be passing overhead at the time.

Nearly the entire sky is seen in this view taken from an orbiting infrared telescope. The bright band is the Milky Way, with the center of the Galaxy at the center of the picture. Hotter materials appear yellow or

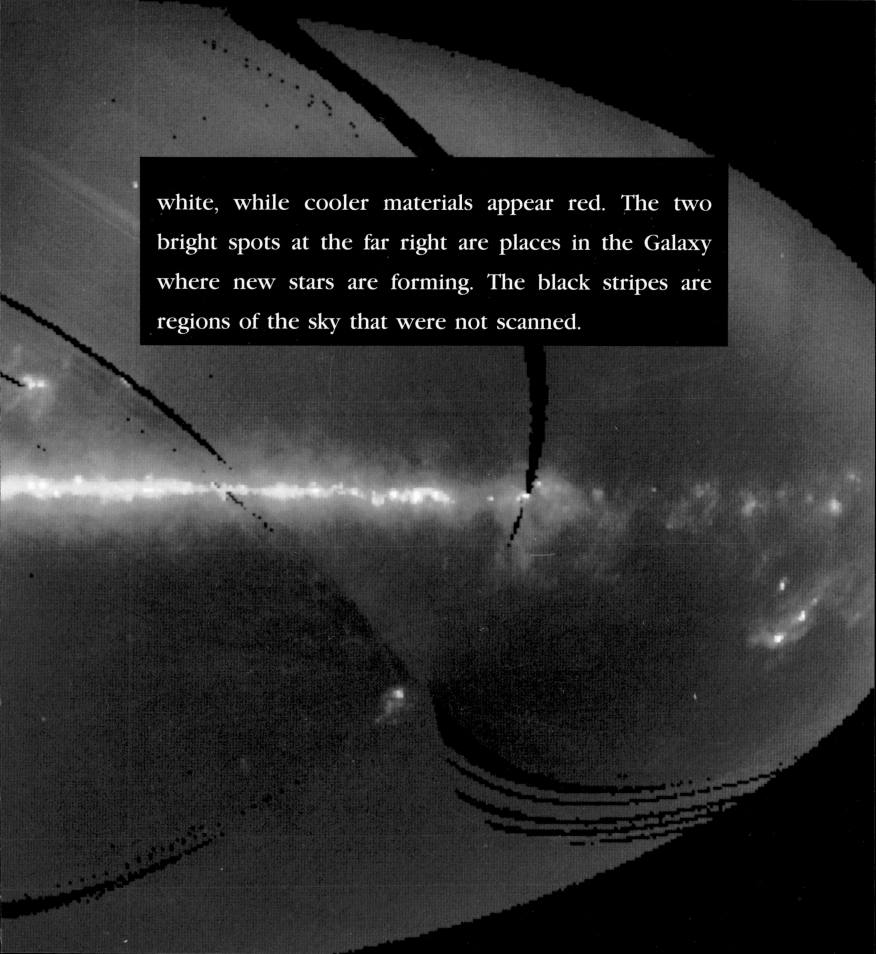

white, while cooler materials appear red. The two bright spots at the far right are places in the Galaxy where new stars are forming. The black stripes are regions of the sky that were not scanned.

If you could see the great spiral of the Milky Way galaxy from a distance, it would look much like these views of other spiral galaxies. It looks like a flat disk of stars with a bulge at the center. The stars in the flat disk are mostly in "arms" that curve out from the central nucleus.

Nucleus

Sun and
Solar System

30,000 light-years

50,000 light-years

Nucleus

Sun and Solar System

Distances in outer space are too great to measure in miles, so space scientists measure with the light-year. A light-year is the distance that light travels in one year — about six trillion miles. If you were in a plane going at five hundred miles per hour, it would take you more than one million years to travel just one light-year.

The Galaxy has three spiral arms. The sun and Solar System are near the inner edge of one of the arms, about thirty thousand light-years from the Galaxy's center. The arms rotate around the center of the Galaxy. The sun travels at a speed of over 600 thousand miles per hour, drawing Earth and the rest of the Solar System along with it. Even at that speed, it takes the sun 225 million years to make the long voyage around the center of the Galaxy.

As immense and important as our galaxy seems to us, it is still only one of about thirty nearby galaxies called the Local Group. Most of the galaxies are clustered around the two chief members of the group: our galaxy and the Andromeda galaxy. The Andromeda galaxy is a galaxy much like ours but slightly larger. It is the nearest large galaxy to us, about 2.2 million light-years distant. At its center is a black hole, millions of times more massive than the Sun.

More than three hundred billion stars make up the Andromeda galaxy. If you were to count one star per second nonstop, it would take you more than nine thousand years to count the stars in that galaxy. The stars that you see sprinkled around the photo are actually in our own galaxy, like raindrops on a windowpane seen against a distant view. The fuzzy, bright object is a satellite galaxy of Andromeda, containing many millions of stars.

Our galaxy also has two smaller satellite galaxies, called the Magellanic Clouds. They are visible to the unaided eye from Earth's southern hemisphere. The fuzzy blue cloud on the right is the Large Magellanic Cloud; the one on the left is the Small Magellanic Cloud. The clouds were named after Ferdinand Magellan, the sixteenth-century Portuguese explorer who saw them when he led the first expedition to sail around the world.

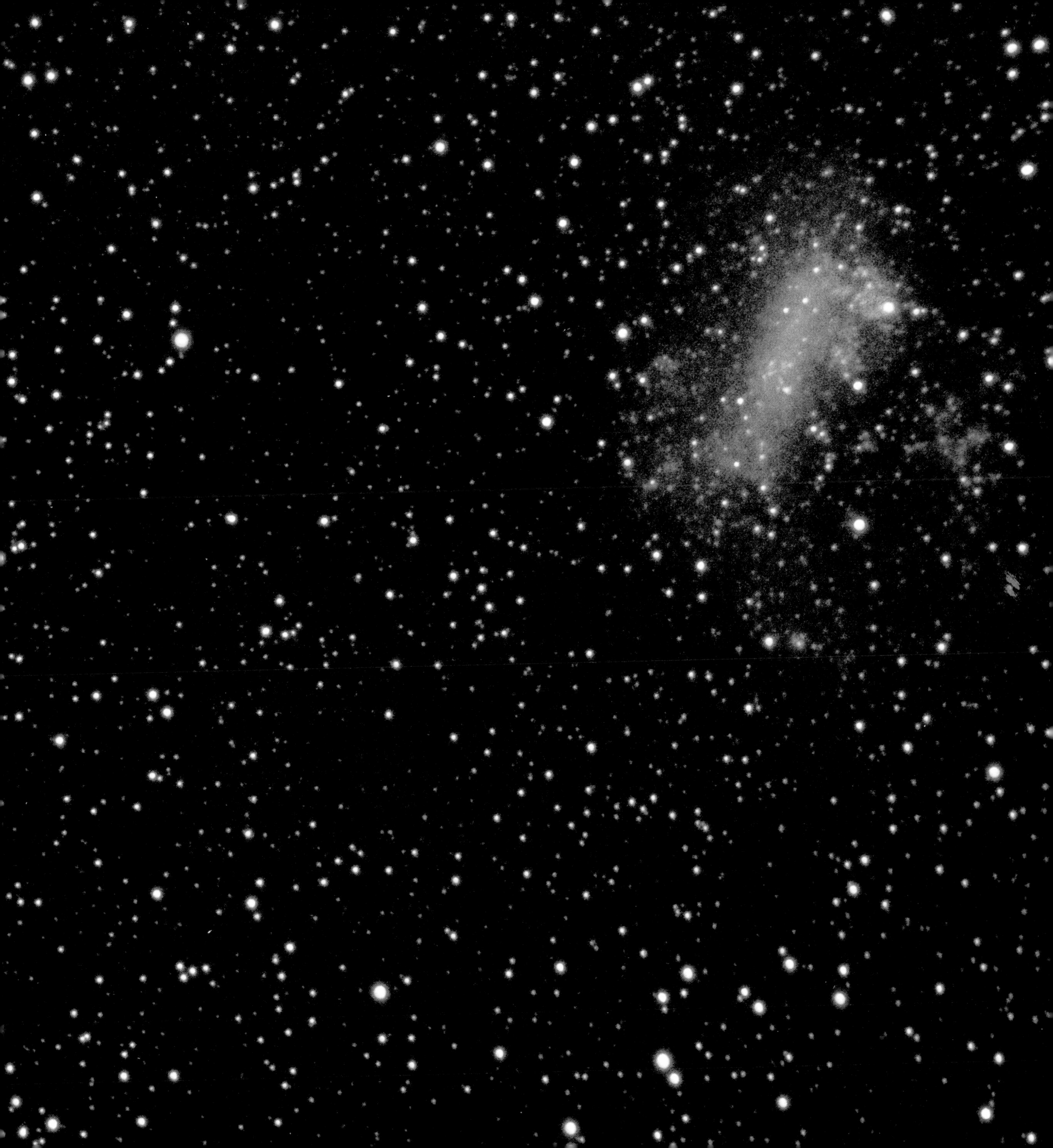

The Large Magellanic Cloud is the galaxy nearest to our own, about 170 thousand light-years away. About one-quarter the size of our galaxy, the Large Magellanic Cloud contains about 15 billion stars and other interesting space objects.

The reddish puff of gas at one end of the cloud (center left) is the huge Tarantula nebula. It is an enormous cloud of dust and gas about eight hundred light-years across, the largest nebula known.

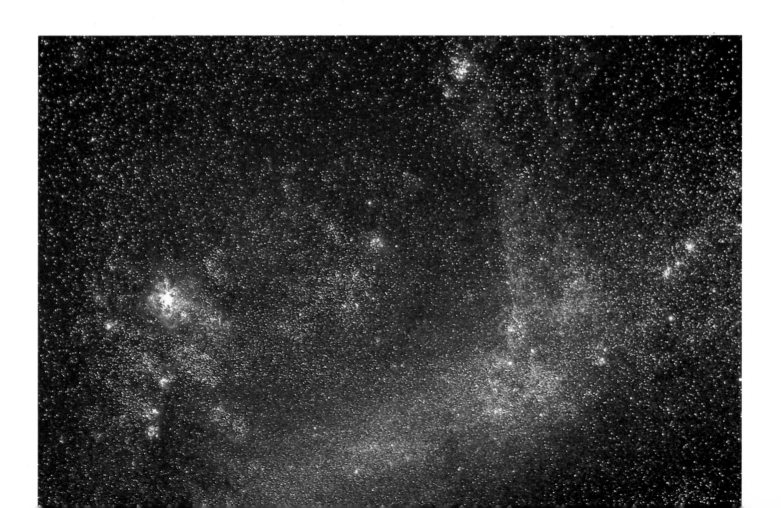

The Large Cloud is also the home of an exploding star that blazed into view in February 1987. It is a supernova, a gigantic star that explodes and flings huge amounts of energy into space for a short time and then dies. For the present, the exploding star is simply called Supernova 1987A. The closest supernova seen from Earth since 1604, it is clearly visible in the night sky over the Southern Hemisphere.

The Small Magellanic Cloud is about two hundred thousand light-years from our galaxy and has about five billion stars. Altogether, the Small and Large Clouds and the other galaxies in the Local Group contain about fifteen hundred billion stars, yet our galactic neighborhood is hardly crowded. The distance across the Local Group is about five million light-years. If a light-year were one inch, then our galaxy would be one and one-half miles across, and the Local Group of galaxies would fit inside a mostly empty eighty-mile-wide stadium.

Scientists class galaxies by their shape after a method first suggested in 1925 by an American astronomer, Edwin Hubble. Hubble identified three main types of galaxies: spirals, ellipticals, and barred spirals. Irregular-shaped galaxies and dwarf galaxies are two kinds that were added later. The photograph shows M74, a spiral galaxy.

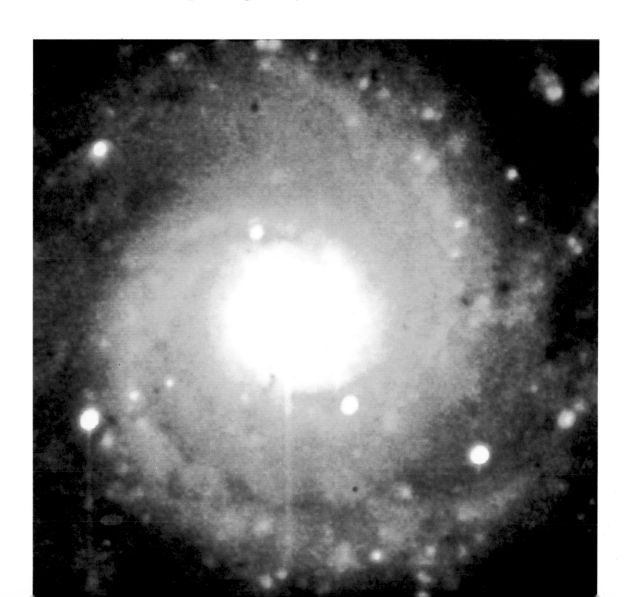

This is M104, a spiral galaxy known as the "Sombrero galaxy" for its appearance. Spiral galaxies are probably formed from giant clouds of rapidly spinning hydrogen gas. Some of the gas is pulled into the center by gravity and condenses into stars. The remainder of the gas rotates around the center, slowly forming new stars. The rotating disk of gas and stars forms arms and gives the galaxy its spiral shape.

Elliptical galaxies far outnumber spiral galaxies. An elliptical galaxy looks like a squashed ball. This is Centaurus A, an elliptical galaxy. It is one of the brightest and largest galaxies known, with three times as many stars as our galaxy. Scientists think that the center of this galaxy is experiencing giant explosions of millions of stars, hurling out clouds of hot gas. The dark band is a thick ring of dust and gas hiding our view of the central region.

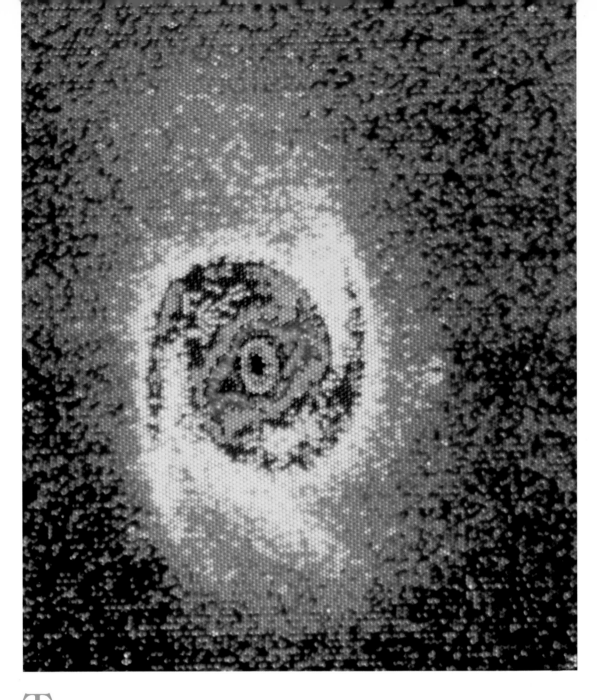

This is a barred spiral galaxy. The photo has been computer-colored to show small details in the galaxy. Barred spiral galaxies have a clear central bar from which the spiral arms trail.

Two galaxies appear in this computer-colored photograph. The larger one is a spiral known as the "Cocoon galaxy" because of its shape. The smaller one just above it is an irregular galaxy. Irregular galaxies are usually smaller than spirals and have no definite shape. The Smaller Magellanic Cloud is a dwarf, irregular galaxy. Dwarf galaxies are small, dim galaxies.

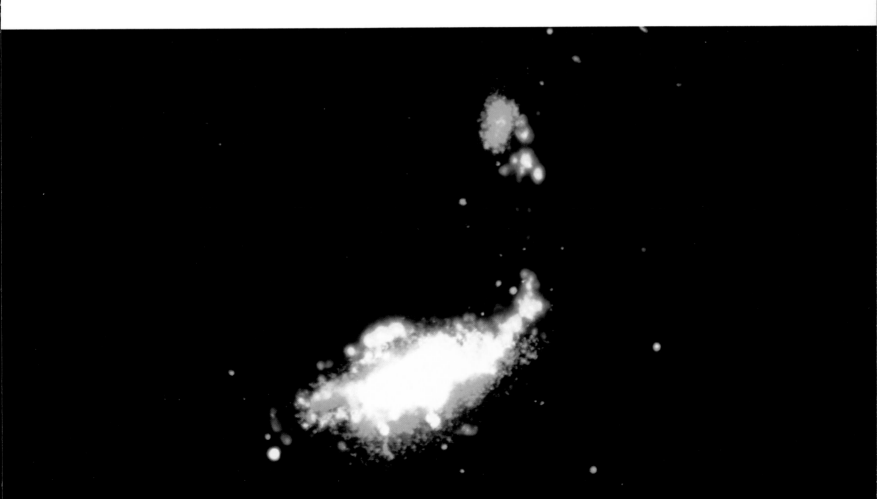

The Southern Ring galaxy is seen in the sky near the Large Magellanic Cloud. Once thought to be part of the Large Cloud, the Ring galaxy is now known to be 270 million light-years away, far beyond the Local Group.

Scientists think that ring galaxies are formed when a large spiral galaxy collides with a smaller galaxy. The ring is formed by the galactic shock wave of the

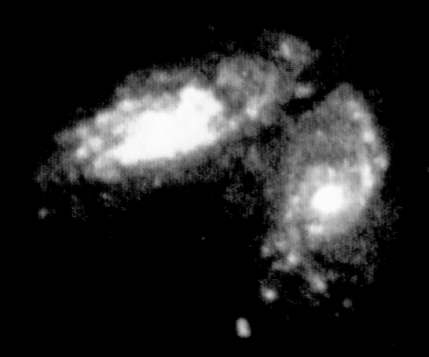

collision, something like the circular ripple a falling rock makes in the water of a pond.

Sometimes a galaxy will change shape only slightly when it brushes by another galaxy. These galaxies in the constellation Virgo have been nicknamed the "Siamese Twins." This pair of spiral galaxies will slowly change shape as they pull apart from each other.

Galaxies seem to group together in space. Several thousand galaxy clusters have been found in all directions in space. Our Local Group of thirty galaxies is only a small cluster. An average cluster contains about 150 galaxies and spreads over 15 million light-years.

Some clusters are even larger. What look like fuzzy stars in this photograph are actually some of the more than one thousand large galaxies and ten thousand dwarf galaxies in the Coma cluster. The galaxies in the Coma cluster are much more densely packed together than the galaxies in the Local Group.

Scientists think that the Coma cluster is part of a supercluster of more than twenty-five hundred major galaxies. Superclusters are large groups of clusters stretched out or torn apart as they move away from one another. Our Local Group itself is part of a Local Supercluster of groups of galaxies.

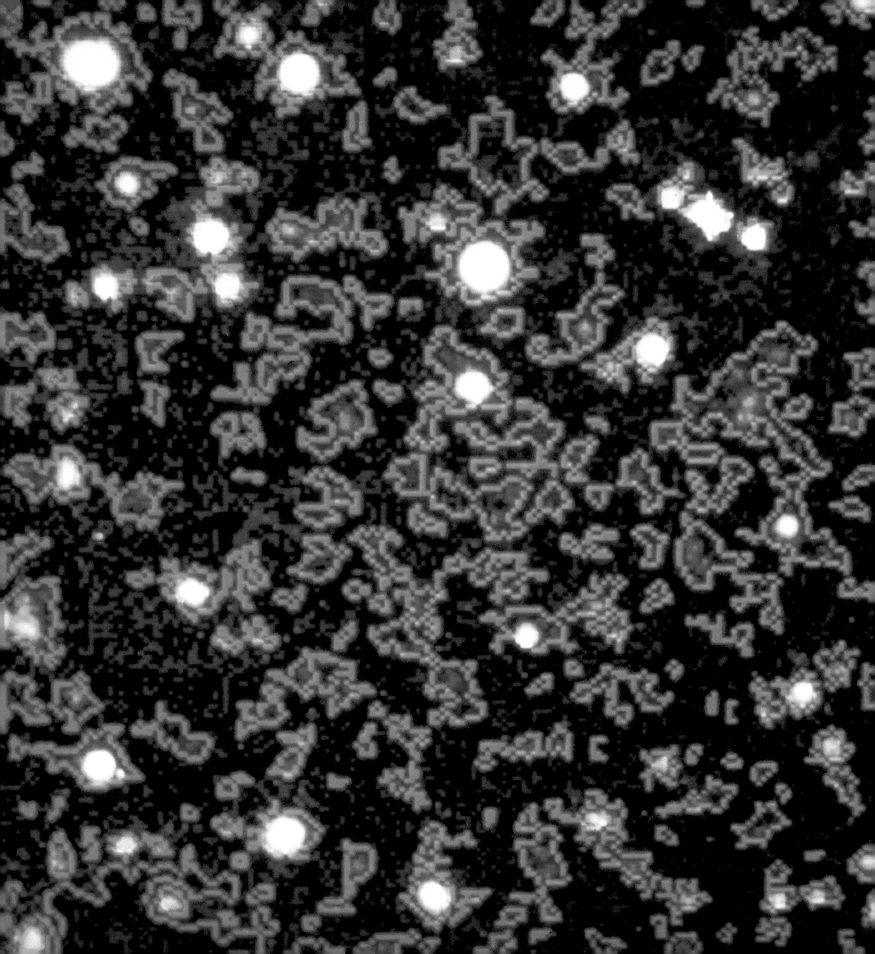

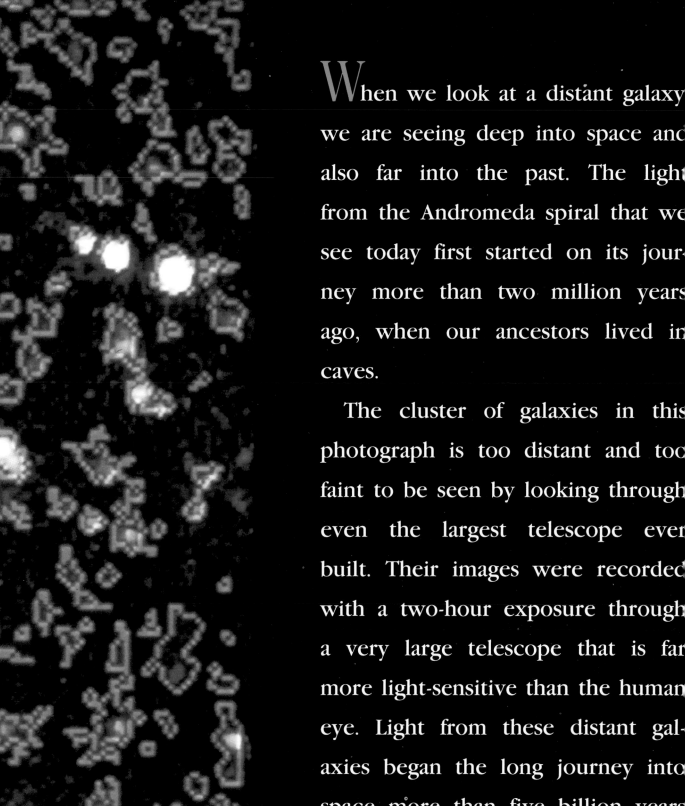

When we look at a distant galaxy, we are seeing deep into space and also far into the past. The light from the Andromeda spiral that we see today first started on its journey more than two million years ago, when our ancestors lived in caves.

The cluster of galaxies in this photograph is too distant and too faint to be seen by looking through even the largest telescope ever built. Their images were recorded with a two-hour exposure through a very large telescope that is far more light-sensitive than the human eye. Light from these distant galaxies began the long journey into space more than five billion years ago, before our planet was born.

How many galaxies are there in the universe? Does the universe have an end? No one knows. This map plots the locations of one million galaxies. But for every galaxy pictured here, there may be ten thousand more galaxies yet unknown. Scientists think that there may be one hundred billion galaxies in our expanding universe. The universe itself is without a boundary, so that one can travel at the speed of light forever without reaching an edge.

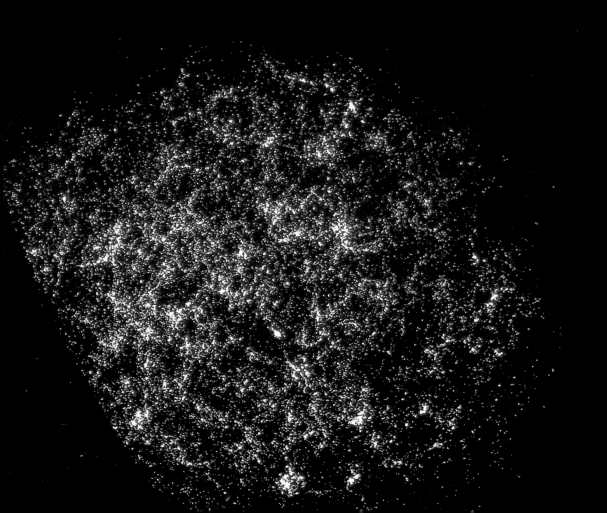